Nadine,
My Funny and Trusty Guide Dog

Nadine,

My Funny and Trusty Guide Dog

By Carol Chiodo Fleischman
Illustrated by Stephanie Ford

PELICAN PUBLISHING COMPANY
GRETNA 2015

For my mother, Irma; Don; and The Seeing Eye
—C. C. F.

The word "Pelican" and the depiction of a pelican are
trademarks of Pelican Publishing Company, Inc., and are
registered in the U.S. Patent and Trademark Office.

Library of Congress Cataloging-in-Publication Data

Fleischman, Carol Chiodo.
  Nadine, my funny and trusty guide dog / by Carol Chiodo Fleischman ;
illustrated by Stephanie Ford.
    pages cm
  Audience: K to Grade 3.
   ISBN 978-1-4556-1927-6 (hardcover : alk. paper) -- ISBN 978-1-4556-
1928-3 (e-book) 1. Guide dogs--Juvenile literature. I. Ford, Stephanie ;
illustrator. II. Title.
  HV1780.2.F54 2014
  362.4'18--dc23
                                   2013051167

Printed in Malaysia
Published by Pelican Publishing Company, Inc.
1000 Burmaster Street, Gretna, Louisiana 70053

Nadine, My Funny and Trusty Guide Dog

My guide dog, Nadine, can be a little clown. Though she completed a lot of training to become a working dog, Nadine can get into mischief.

One morning soon after I came home from the guide dog school, I woke up and stepped down on the cold floor. My foot brushed over a soft lump, so I picked it up. Phew! Were these dirty socks? I guessed right.

Then I stepped on a balled up t-shirt—a stinky t-shirt. My nose wrinkled from the sour smell. Why were all my dirty clothes on the floor?

I suspected Nadine had pulled them out of the laundry basket. Instead of using crumbs like Hansel and Gretel, she made a trail of clothes for me to follow in the house. That little jokester licked my hand as I grabbed my white cane. I swept the tip along the floor from side to side to find each piece. This four-legged shadow followed along at my heels, panting as she walked. Was she laughing at me? Soon, I got the clothes back into the hamper.

As I sat at my kitchen table, I thought about the last few weeks we spent training together. At the guide dog school, a dog trainer taught us how to stay safe. "Use your hearing, and your dog will see for you," he said. "Think like a team."

Today, for the first time, we'd be walking alone. We needed to find our own way in my neighborhood. In the kitchen, I called, "Come girl!" Nadine padded along the wooden floor toward me, where I waited with her harness in my hand. "Go inside," I told her. Nadine should have slid her head into the leather straps so I could close the buckle. Instead, she lowered her head. Then my dog changed her mind. Before I could fasten her in the harness, Nadine wriggled away.

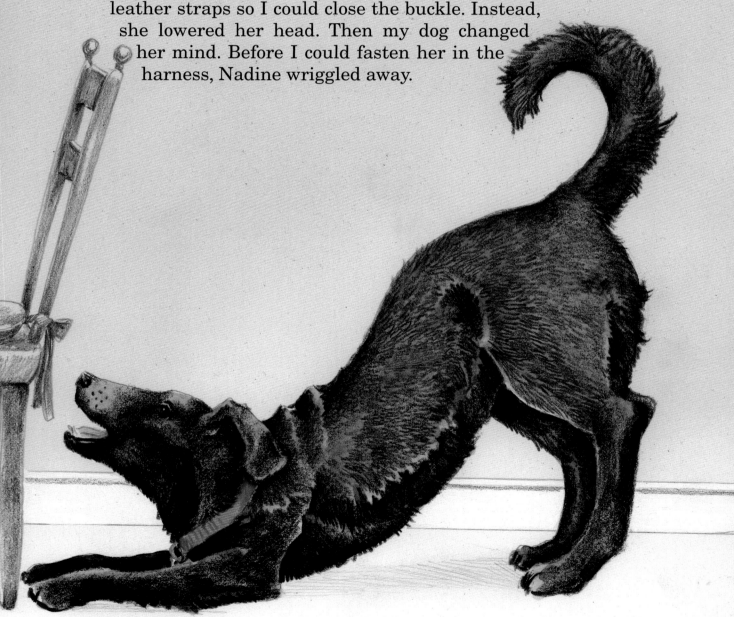

Nadine's toenails clicked along the floor to the table. That silly dog must be hiding beneath it. "Now she wants to play hide and seek," I thought. I wanted to laugh out loud, but I knew I shouldn't. Since it was time for her to work, I had to focus and think of a way to get Nadine to come to me.

I walked over to the kitchen cabinet and reached into the tall box of dog treats. When Nadine saw me put some treats into my jacket pocket, she came out of hiding. Guide dogs know they will get a reward for good work. Now Nadine was ready to guide me.

Finally, we made it outside, and our bodies swayed easily as we began to walk. "This is like dancing!" I smiled. My neighbor called to me from his yard. "The weatherman on TV warned that a storm is coming," he said. "Better not be out too long with your new dog." "Thank you," I responded.

His warning didn't stop me. I was having so much fun on this chilly winter day! I sniffed the sweet smell of chimney smoke as we made our way through the neighborhood. On one block, catbirds nesting on a bush were startled as we walked past them. Their squeaks and flapping wings filled the air with sound.

On another block, my mouth watered. I smelled fresh dough baking at the pizzeria. "Ping, ping!" The flag flapping in the school yard told me we had walked a long distance. The fresh air made me feel good, but that feeling didn't last long.

Soon the wind grew stronger, so I pulled my collar up. Tree limbs quivered, dumping clumps of snow on us. Nadine shook to get the snow off her fur. Cold snowflakes stung my cheeks, and my fingers felt numb. "Let's go home, girl," I said, wrapping my scarf tighter around my neck.

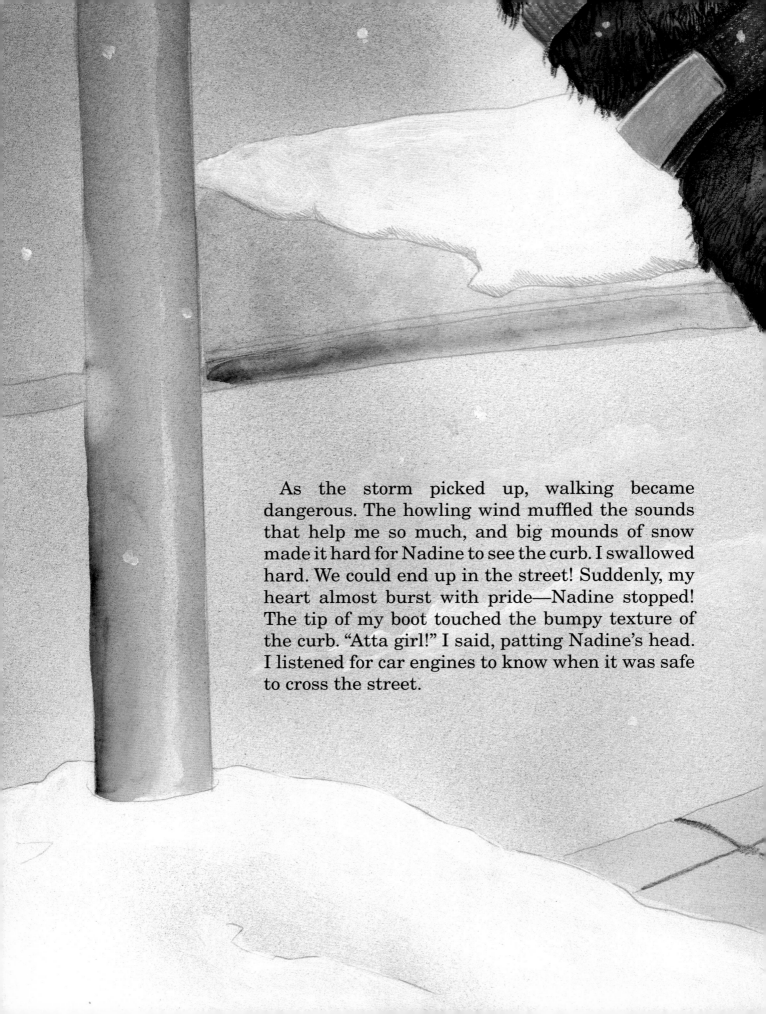

As the storm picked up, walking became dangerous. The howling wind muffled the sounds that help me so much, and big mounds of snow made it hard for Nadine to see the curb. I swallowed hard. We could end up in the street! Suddenly, my heart almost burst with pride—Nadine stopped! The tip of my boot touched the bumpy texture of the curb. "Atta girl!" I said, patting Nadine's head. I listened for car engines to know when it was safe to cross the street.

I pulled my scarf off my ears to hear the traffic better. I gave Nadine a command to walk when things were quiet, but she wouldn't move. "Forward," I repeated. Then I remembered the advice of the dog trainer. "Trust your dog," he told us. I took a deep breath and listened again. "Zoom!" I heard a car whiz past us. Nadine was right to disobey me! She saw the danger I could not see.

I grabbed the harness tighter and gave Nadine the command again. This time she obeyed and moved ahead. At the opposite curb, her strong shoulders pulled hard. I heard a sound clink and clang like metal. We squeezed close together and Nadine led me around something. Was it a garbage can rolling past us?

On my left, I heard a creaking sound. "That must be an open gate swaying in the storm," I thought. The wind was as mean as a bully, pushing us along. Nadine slowed down to warn me that we were walking over an icy patch. A dog barked and barked at us, but she did not become distracted.

Finally, I heard a soft tinkle. I turned my head this way and that so I could listen carefully. The sound of the wind chimes on our porch seemed as beautiful as church bells. "We did it!" I exclaimed. We were home and we were safe.

Inside our warm house, I took Nadine's harness off and gave her a big hug. I sat down to pull off my wet boots and soggy socks. Nadine nudged my pocket. "Oh my, I almost forgot your treat," I said. I gave her a dog biscuit and heard her crunch each bite. Then I reached down to pick up my wet socks, but they were gone! My trusty guide was being a little clown again. Now where did Nadine hide my socks?

Author's Note

Many litters of puppies are born at The Seeing Eye, a guide dog school in New Jersey. A pup must be intelligent and have a gentle temperament for its job as a guide. At about eight weeks old, the puppy goes to live with a foster family. During this time, the puppy learns basic obedience and good manners, including staying off furniture. The person responsible for the dog is called the "puppy raiser." Soon, the pup matures into a dog that sits quietly under the table during family mealtime. Since the dog can go everywhere with its blind owner, it must learn to behave in public. Then, it is ready to go on to the next part of training.

After one year, the dog returns to The Seeing Eye. The trainer and pup work together every day for four months. The pup is taught to walk on the trainer's left side, with the harness in the trainer's left hand. This will allow the future blind owner to have a free hand to open doors or carry packages. At this stage, the dog learns to avoid an obstacle, like a bike or tree branch, blocking the sidewalk. Stopping at the curb is another important lesson. The guide dog waits to hear the command "forward" before crossing the street.

Next, a blind student arrives at the school to stay for about twenty-five days. During this time, the dog trainer evaluates the person's pace. Does he walk fast or slowly? Does he need a dog that pulls hard or more gently? Will the team walk on city sidewalks or on country roads? From the dogs he has taught, the trainer matches a dog to each student.

Each day, the student and his dog take walks. The dog trainer goes along, following behind like a coach and making helpful suggestions. "Remember to praise your dog," he might say. A dog that graduates from The Seeing Eye school is called a Seeing Eye® dog. All other trained dogs that help the blind are called guide dogs.

A guide dog's purpose is to lead his owner safely when walking. As the team travels together, a blind person must use his hearing while the dog uses its sight. All trained guide dogs wear a special harness when they are in public. It is important not to speak to or pet a working dog so the guide dog is not distracted.